Date: 2/13/15

J 948.1 MUR
Murray, Julie,
Norway/

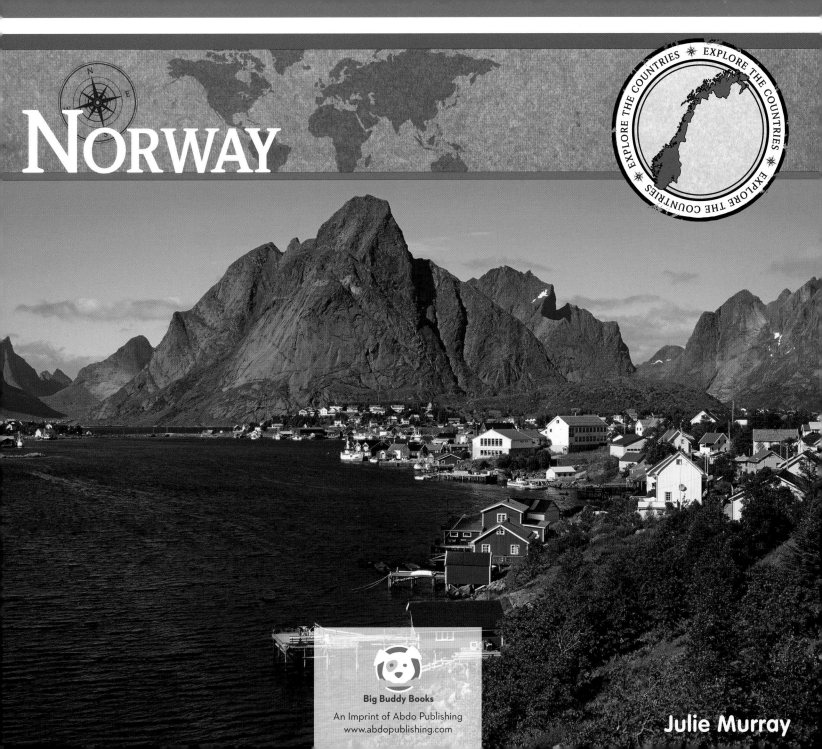

NORWAY

Big Buddy Books
An Imprint of Abdo Publishing
www.abdopublishing.com

Julie Murray

www.abdopublishing.com

Published by Abdo Publishing, a division of ABDO, PO Box 398166, Minneapolis, Minnesota 55439.
Copyright © 2015 by Abdo Consulting Group, Inc. International copyrights reserved in all countries. No part
of this book may be reproduced in any form without written permission from the publisher. Big Buddy Books™
is a trademark and logo of Abdo Publishing.

Printed in the United States of America, North Mankato, Minnesota.
032014
092014

Cover Photo: Glow Images.
Interior Photos: ASSOCIATED PRESS (pp. 17, 19, 33), Getty Images (pp. 15, 33), Glow Images (pp. 13, 23,
    29, 35), iStockphoto (pp. 21, 27, 38), Mondadori via Getty Images (p. 31), Shutterstock (pp. 5, 9, 11, 16,
    19, 21, 25, 34, 35, 37, 38), Time & Life Pictures/Getty Images (p. 13).

Coordinating Series Editor: Rochelle Baltzer
Editor: Sarah Tieck
Contributing Editors: Megan M. Gunderson, Marcia Zappa
Graphic Design: Adam Craven

Country population and area figures taken from the CIA World Factbook.

Library of Congress Cataloging-in-Publication Data

Murray, Julie, 1969-
 Norway / Julie Murray.
    pages cm. -- (Explore the countries)
 ISBN 978-1-62403-345-2
 1. Norway--Juvenile literature. I. Title.
 DL409.M875 2014
 948.1--dc23
                              2013048627

NORWAY

CONTENTS

AROUND THE WORLD

Our world has many countries. Each country has beautiful land. It has its own rich history. And, the people have their own languages and ways of life.

Norway is a country in Europe. What do you know about Norway? Let's learn more about this place and its story!

 Did You Know?

Norway's official language is Norwegian. Sami is also official in some areas.

The Borgund church was built around 1150. It is a special style of wooden church.

Passport to Norway

Norway is a country in northern Europe. Three countries border it. It is also bordered by bodies of water.

Norway's total area is 125,021 square miles (323,802 sq km). More than 5.1 million people live there.

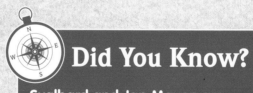

Did You Know?

Svalbard and Jan Mayen are island territories of Norway. They are located in the Arctic Ocean.

WHERE IN THE WORLD?

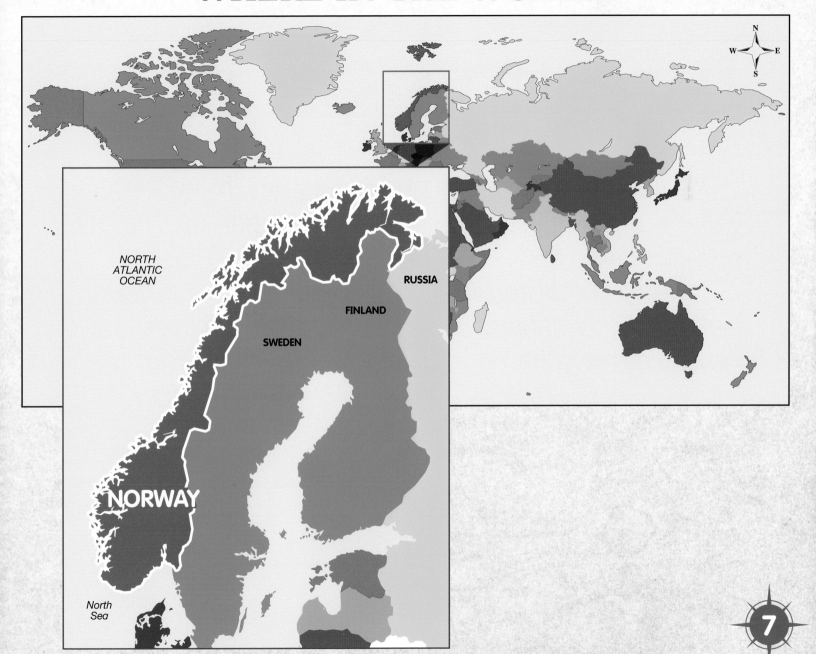

IMPORTANT CITIES

Oslo is Norway's **capital** and largest city. More than 613,000 people live in the city and nearby areas. The city is on the Oslo Fjord.

Oslo is a center for business and the arts. It has one of Norway's largest ports. The city has a railroad hub, too. People visit Frogner Park and the University of Oslo.

SAY IT

Oslo
AHZ-loh

fjord
fee-AWRD

NORWAY

Trondheim

Bergen

Oslo

The Oslo area is known for its beautiful forests and lakes.

Bergen is Norway's second-largest city. This city and its nearby areas are home to more than 263,000 people. Bergen is at the head of By Fjord. Fish products and machinery ship from its port.

Trondheim is Norway's third-largest city. More than 176,000 people live in the city and its nearby areas. It is located on Trondheims Fjord and the Nid River. Fish, wood products, copper, and iron ores ship from the city.

Bergen is known for its historic wooden buildings.

The Nidaros Cathedral was built in Trondheim in the 1100s.

Norway in History

People have lived in Norway for more than 10,000 years. One of the earliest groups was the Sami. The Sami moved from place to place with reindeer herds. They hunted and fished for food.

Beginning in the late 700s, Viking tribes lived in what is now Norway. They sailed in longboats to explore new lands. They often stole things and attacked people.

SAY IT

Sami
SAH-mee

Today, some Sami still herd reindeer.

Vikings sailed to new lands. Erik the Red was a Viking explorer who was born in Norway.

Over the years, Norway was ruled by Sweden and Denmark. In 1814, Sweden took control of the land. Norway agreed to be ruled by Sweden's king, but kept its own government. Still, people wanted to separate from Sweden. So in 1905, Norway became independent.

Norway worked to grow into a strong country. But, there were many times when people had no jobs or the country struggled. Today, Norway's **economy** is strong. And, its government makes sure that all people are cared for.

In 1905, King Haakon VII began ruling Norway.

J. Russell & Sons.

TIMELINE

1299

Akershus Castle was built in Oslo. It is still used today.

Around 900

Harald I became Norway's first king. He was also called Harald Fairhair.

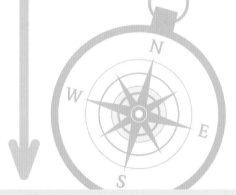

1825

Sondre Norheim was born in southern Norway. He came up with new ski bindings that changed the sport of skiing. These allowed skiers to have more control and do more turns.

1928

Figure skater Sonja Henie of Oslo won her first Olympic gold medal. She won more Olympic and world titles in skating than any other woman.

1876

Composer Edvard Grieg's songs for the play *Peer Gynt* were played for the first time. "Morning Mood" and "In the Hall of the Mountain King" are two famous songs.

2011

Terrorist attacks in Oslo and a nearby island killed 77 people. They were the country's deadliest since the 1940s.

An Important Symbol

Norway's flag was adopted in 1898. The background is red. In the center is a blue cross outlined in white.

Norway's government is a **constitutional monarchy**. A group called the Storting makes laws. The prime minister is the head of government. The king or queen is the head of state.

Norway's flag was designed in 1821, when the country was ruled by Sweden. The Swedish king did not allow Norway to use it for 77 years.

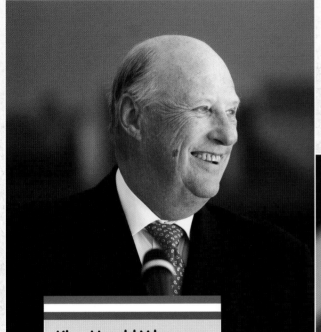

King Harald V became Norway's king in 1991.

Erna Solberg became Norway's prime minister in 2013.

ACROSS THE LAND

Norway is known for its beautiful land. Long ago, **glaciers** formed deep valleys and narrow bays called fjords. The country has rocky coasts. And, there are mountains and forests. There is also farmland.

Norway has lakes, waterfalls, rivers, and islands. The Lofoten Islands are off the northwest coast.

Did You Know?

In January, Oslo's average high temperature is about 32°F (0°C). In July, it is 71°F (22°C).

Northern Norway is known as "the land of the midnight sun." There, the sun does not set on certain days in the summer. That's because it is above the Arctic Circle.

Norway still has glaciers. Some people hike and climb them.

Norway's animals include reindeer, beavers, and lemmings. Its birds include puffins, snowy owls, and cranes. Trout, salmon, whales, and seals live in the water.

The country's land is home to thousands of different plants. Wild berries and flowering plants such as heather grow there. There are birch, asp, and pine trees. Some parts of Norway are too cold for many trees to grow.

Both male and female reindeer grow antlers. They have heavy coats that keep them warm in cold areas.

EARNING A LIVING

Norway has a strong **economy**. Many people have education, government, or health care jobs. Norway's factories make products from metal and oil. They also make food and build ships.

Norway's water is one of its major **natural resources**. It provides cod and haddock. Oil and natural gas are found in the North Sea. And, mountain rivers provide power.

Did You Know?

Farmers grow barley, wheat, and oats. They raise chickens, pigs, and cattle.

Shipbuilding and shipping are important businesses in Norway.

LIFE IN NORWAY

Norway's people live in both **rural** areas and cities. The country is known for its high standard of living. People work hard and enjoy spending time outside.

Norwegians usually eat four meals a day. The main meal often includes fish, boiled potatoes, and vegetables. The other three meals often include open-faced sandwiches.

Did You Know?

In Norway, children must attend school from ages 6 to 16.

Seafood is popular in Norway. Herring is a favorite sandwich topping.

Lefse is a soft Norwegian flatbread. People may eat it with butter and sugar.

Norwegians love to fish, swim, hike, and sail. Skiing is the national sport. Ice skating is also popular. Soccer and bandy, a type of hockey, are popular team sports.

The Evangelical Lutheran Church is Norway's official church. The church is based on the teachings of Martin Luther. However, people are free to choose any religion.

Many Norwegians learn to ski as children. Some begin learning as early as age two or three!

FAMOUS FACES

Henrik Ibsen was born in the town of Skien on March 20, 1828. He wrote plays. His work remains important in theaters around the world.

Ibsen wrote his first play around 1850. He became known for his sad, bold stories. His most famous plays include *A Doll's House* and *Hedda Gabler*. Ibsen died in 1906.

Did You Know?

Ibsen's major plays are often set in Norway.

Ibsen printed 25 plays during his life.

Edvard Munch was born on December 12, 1863, in Löten. He became one of Norway's most famous artists. Munch used color and shapes to show feelings in his work. One of his most famous paintings is *The Scream*. He painted it in 1893. Munch died in 1944.

Did You Know?

The Munch Museum is in Oslo.

The Scream shows Munch's unusual painting style.

Munch's paintings changed over the years. At first he painted about feelings. Later, he painted more about nature and color.

33

TOUR BOOK

Imagine traveling to Norway! Here are some places you could go and things you could do.

 **Explore**

Take a boat cruise to see Sogn Fjord. It is Norway's longest and deepest fjord.

 See

Hike to the top of Pulpit Rock. It is 1,982 feet (604 m) high. People spend time there taking pictures and having picnics.

 Ride

The Bergen Railway is one of Europe's highest railroads. It crosses mountains between Bergen and Oslo.

Discover

Oslo's Frogner Park is home to the Vigeland Sculpture Park. It has more than 200 sculptures by Norwegian artist Gustav Vigeland.

Learn

The Norwegian Folk Museum in Oslo shows Norway's history. There are more than 150 buildings. The staff dresses in clothes from the past.

A GREAT COUNTRY

The story of Norway is important to our world. It is a land of grand mountains and fjords. It is a country of brave and strong people.

The people and places that make up Norway offer something special. They help make the world a more beautiful, interesting place.

Kjerag is a mountain in southwest Norway. A large rock is stuck there between two cliffs. Many people take pictures standing on the rock!

37

Norway Up Close

Official Name: Kongeriket Norge
(Kingdom of Norway)

Flag:

Population (rank): 5,147,792
(July 2014 est.)
(121st most-populated country)

Total Area (rank): 125,021 square miles
(68th largest country)

Capital: Oslo

Official Languages: Norwegian, Sami

Currency: Norwegian krone

Form of Government: Constitutional
monarchy

National Anthem: "Ja, vi elsker dette
landet" (Yes, We Love This Country)

IMPORTANT WORDS

capital a city where government leaders meet.

composer a person who writes music.

constitutional monarchy (kahnt-stuh-TOO-shnuhl MAH-nuhr-kee) a form of government in which a king or queen has only those powers given by a country's laws and constitution.

economy the way that a country produces, sells, and buys goods and services.

glacier (GLAY-shuhr) a huge chunk of ice and snow on land.

natural resources useful and valued supplies from nature.

rural of or relating to open land away from towns and cities.

terrorist a person who uses violence to scare or control people or governments.

WEBSITES

To learn more about Explore the Countries, visit **booklinks.abdopublishing.com**. These links are routinely monitored and updated to provide the most current information available.

INDEX